I0796094

I wrote a
book about
US

Dear ____________________,

They say write what you know, so that's what I did. I wrote about you, and I wrote about me, and I wrote about us, because... I know us. And I *love us*. What we have is at the top of my list of all the stuff I'm grateful for. What we have makes so many things possible. What we have just makes me look forward to more.

I hope this book becomes one of your favorite things, because you are absolutely one of mine. Over and over. All the time.

Love,

____

Let's start
from the
BEGINNING.

Any BOOK
about US
is GOING TO Be
A BOOK about two
people
who definitely

And just to
Set the
scene...

I want to

HIGHLIGHT THAT TIME WE

Because *moments* like that Define who we ARE to me.

It's just a
little thing, But...

Every time we
it makes me
SO HAPPY.

When it comes to the two of us...

This is our most unbelievable
Similarity:

And this is our biggest
Difference:

I love
all of our
complexities.

What's this?

It's OUR OWN
PERSONAL
JUKEBOX
NO $$ REQUIRED
1.
2.
3.
4.
5.
6.

You and I make a truly Great Team.

If we had a uniform, it would be:

And if we had a motto, it would be:

And if we had a mascot, it would be:

I honestly think...

WITH ENOUGH ______ AND

______

______

AND ______

YOU AND I COULD *really* CHANGE the WORLD for the Better.

I'm so IMPRESSED we *finally* figured out *how to*

It's official.

We're amazing.

REMEMBER that time when I:

and you:

Thank you.

and REMEMBER that other time when you:

and I:

You're welcome.

Okay:
I think I can
finally
ADMiT it:

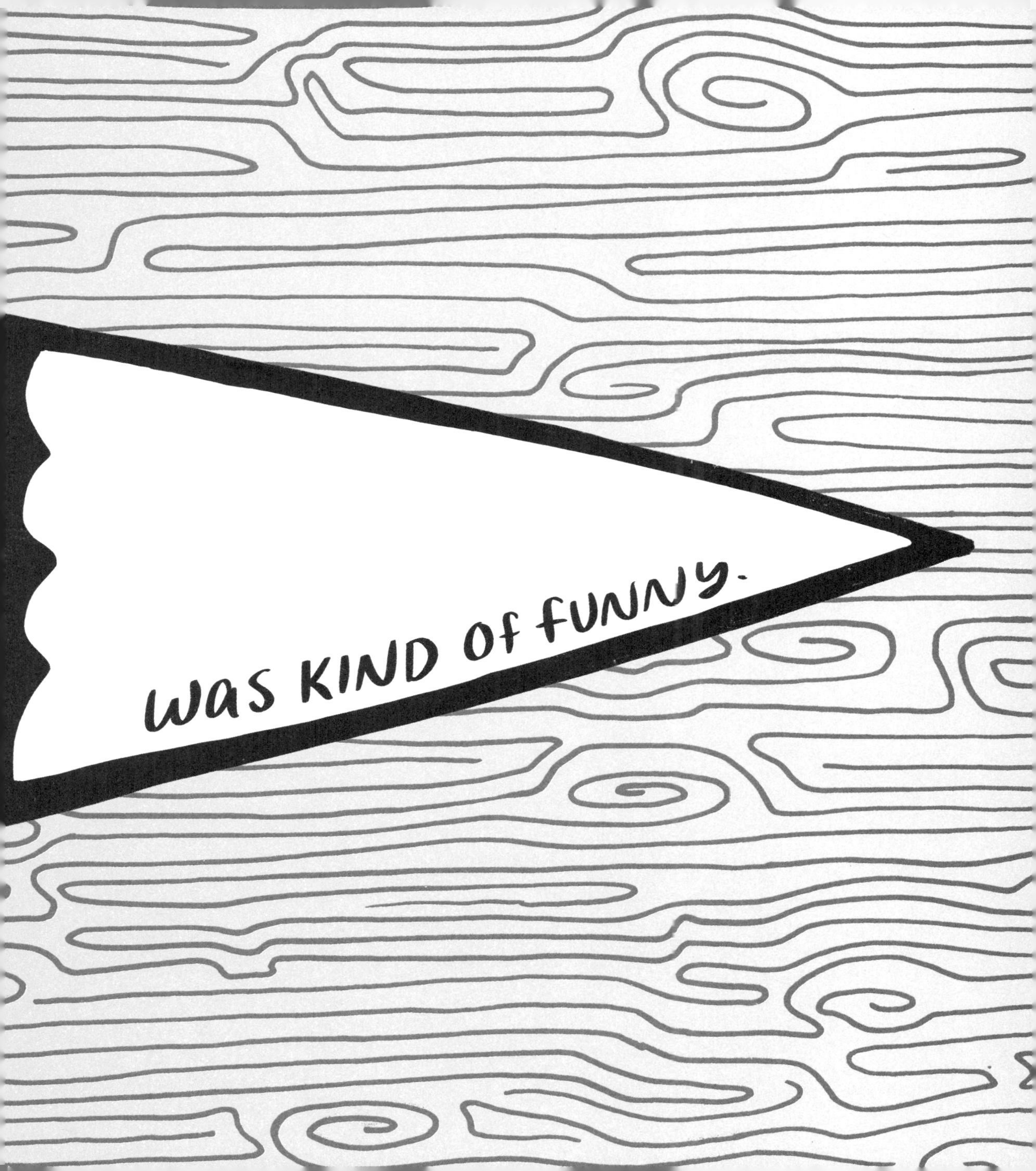
was KIND of funny.

I don't know what the rest of the WORLD thinks...

But I KNOW we
aren't wrong about:

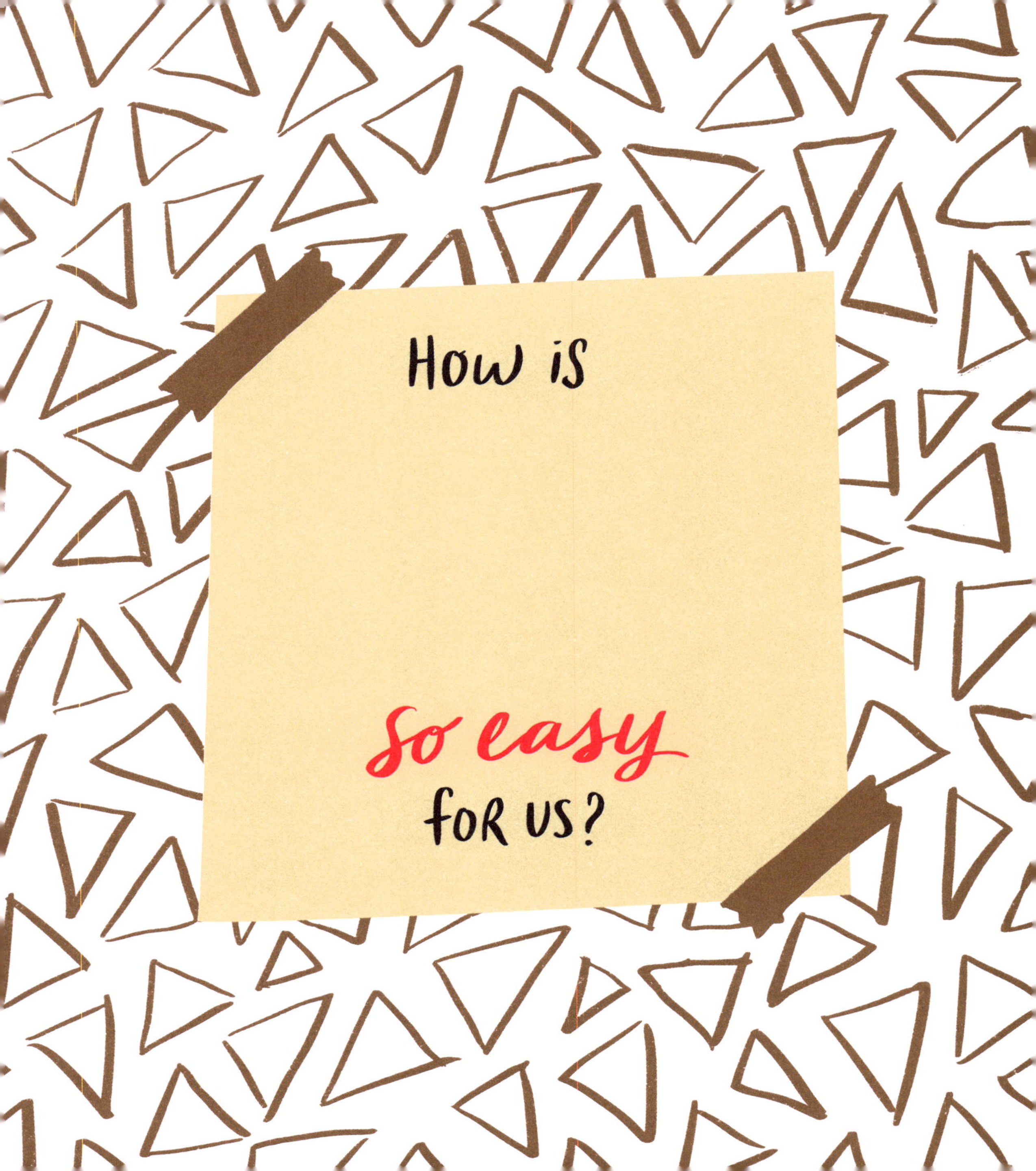
How is
so easy
for us?

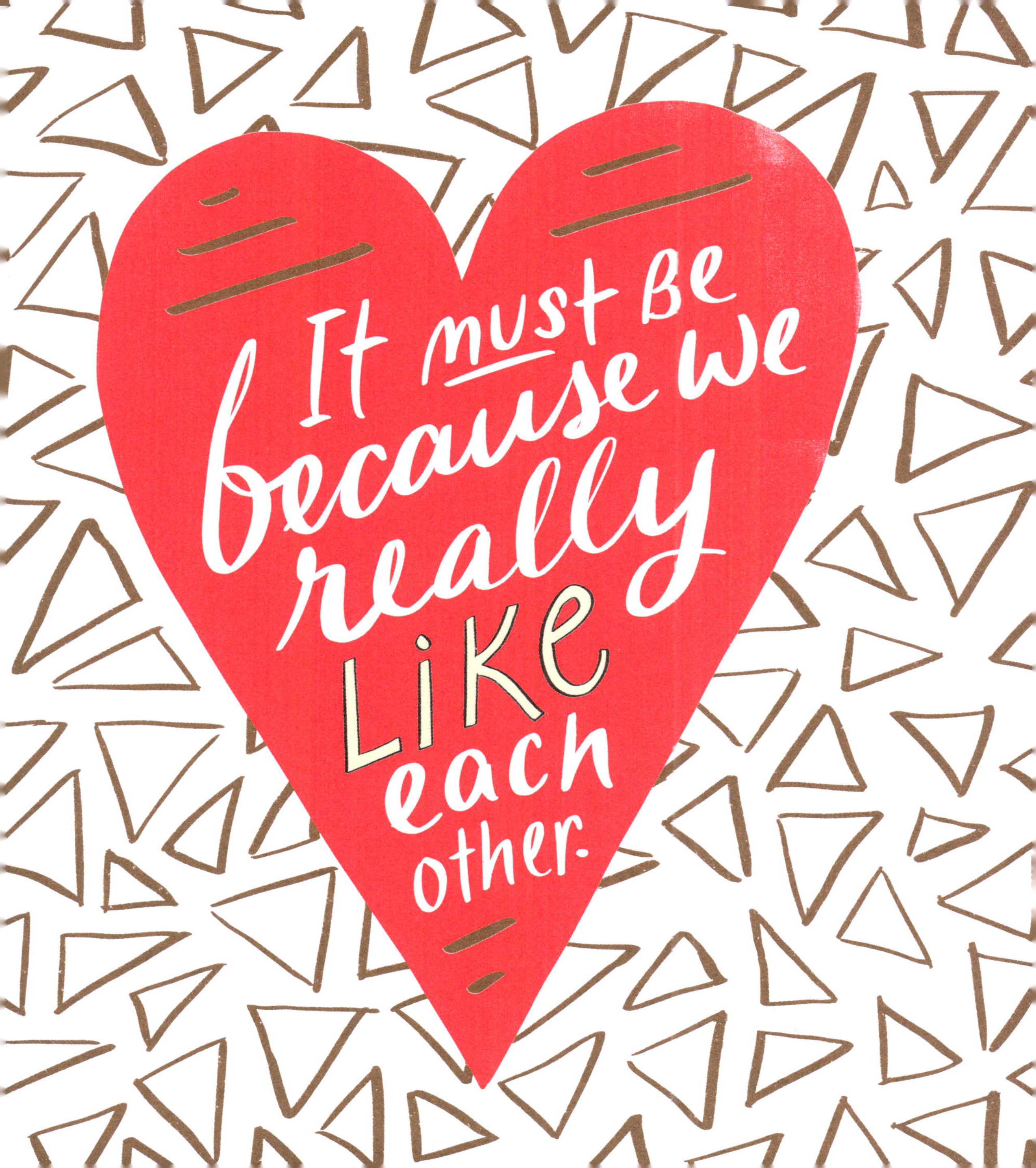
It must be
because we
really
Like
each
other.

Remember that time...

We went to:

And then we:

And:

I'll ***never forget*** that.

I bet a lot of *people* think we're

And you know what?
I'm okay with that.

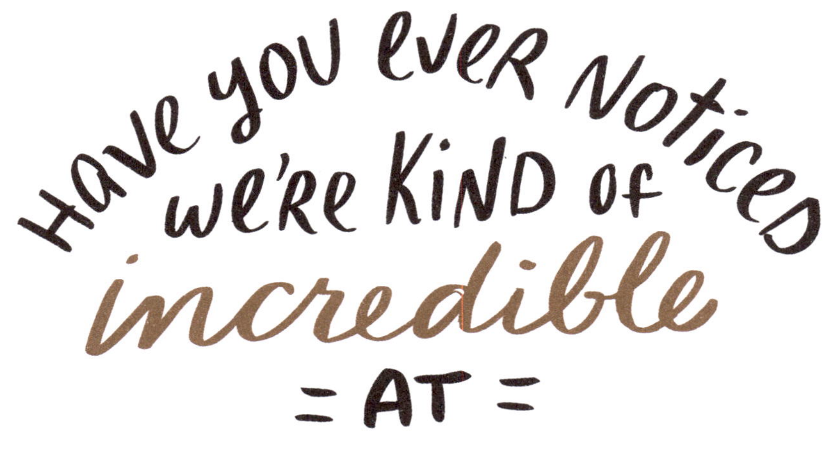
Have you ever noticed
we're kind of
incredible
AT

Is this a

GUINNESS WORLD RECORDS

kind of thing?

maybe we should *try.*

You DON'T think IT'S

weird

that we

Do you?

Oh, GOOD.
Me either.

I think it's *perfect* that

you're so good at

AND I'M SO GOOD AT

BASICALLY, *together* WE'RE UNSTOPPABLE.

It's remarkable that in ALL THE TIME we've known each other, we've only *grown* more and MORE

WOW.

When I LOOK BACK at how we handled

I KNOW WE COULD get through anything.

I'm pretty sure
the stars
BROUGHT
= US =
together
SO WE COULD

How *lucky*
are we?

I'm ABSOLUTELY
certain...

I will never
Get TiReD of
the way we

Remember that DAY we

That will *forever* be one of my favorite memories.

I don't tend to be one to

Predict *the* future,

But if I had to...

I'd Bet we have a lot of

ahead of us.

If I could make **one wish** come true for us...

It would be

In fact, let's consider that wish made.

I hope we are always...

every bit as

as we are

today

WRITTEN BY: M.H. Clark

DESIGNED & ILLUSTRATED BY: Justine Edge

EDITED BY: Ruth Austin

Library of Congress Control Number: 2019949567 | ISBN: 978-1-970147-02-5

10th printing. Printed in China with soy inks on FSC®-Mix certified paper.